Nurturing Kindness

a manifesto for unapologetic self-love and healing

Karin Holmes

Copyright © 2020

All rights reserved. This book or any portion thereof may not be reproduced or used in any manner whatsoever without the express written permission of the author except for the use of brief quotations in a book review.

Printed in Australia. First Printing 2020
ISBN: 978-0-6487529-5-0

*To Kiana and Maisie,
my fierce warrior girls.*

Contents

Welcome	7
Introduction	13
Shame – a sneaky bitch	19
Belonging	37
You are enough	49
Depression	55
Anxiety	75
Self-doubt	91
Self-care	105
Epilogue	123
Glossary	125
About the Author	131

Welcome!

Welcome to Nurturing Kindness! This book has a few purposes and I hope it will help you in many different situations. Most important of all, 'Nurturing Kindness' is a guide and an encouragement to get back to basics.

We live in a world that while heavily connected with each other through social media, is also a world that has created more loneliness, isolation and sadness than ever before. We seem to have forgotten how to be nice and caring to each other and ourselves. Our approach to things and people is viewed through selfish lenses – what can this person do for ME? What use is this job, company, opportunity, friend to ME? We want to be better, stronger, faster and we want it instantly. Our sense of entitlement has grown and has diminished our world of patience, understanding and most sadly – kindness.

A lack of kindness is the root cause for so many issues today. Kindness has become an almost revolutionary concept. We need and deserve stories of random acts of kindness. Now, more than ever, we need to know that good still exists and giving and helping others has not been replaced by selfishness and greed.

Kindness appears to have diminished to the point that it seems we need to educate people about the concept again. The hateful campaigns of a few old, white, rich, conservative males in the media against welfare recipients, low-income earners, the mentally ill and others who are struggling have gained too much attention and ignorant followers. Their campaigns don't allow for kindness and looking out for each other. Much more is to be gained for these old turds by people fighting and being divided. Those faceless manipulators make more money when people are miserable than when we are all happy and settled with our lot.

Kindness only survives where people make an effort to keep it going. It is often easier to give in to greed and other selfish urges. Kindness needs effort at times but not as much as some people want you to believe. That is where 'Nurturing Kindness' comes in. It is a guide to relearn and rediscover kindness and how to live it, share it and grow it. The book focuses on the most important person in this ever-important movement – you.

We can't be kind and caring and helping others if we can't be kind and caring to ourselves first. And no – that is NOT selfish. It is kindness we show to ourselves. That is another important idea that has almost been extinguished by the manipulators in our society. Kind people don't need to listen to propaganda because we can see straight through it. So of course, they don't want us to think that being kind and taking care of ourselves in a caring and loving way is a good thing! After all, the greedy and heartless have much to lose.

Imagine a society where doctors and other healthcare professionals know the worth of a kind word and listening ear – both to patients and each other. How much money would big pharma lose if doctors promoted kind human interaction and connection instead of a pill? How much money would the war industry lose if people would remember kindness before greed and were motivated by kindness and not selfish gains to resolve a conflict?

What if we put the human connection first and treated our bodies with kindness and good food? How much kinder would we treat our planet if we were kinder to ourselves, to begin with?

Worth a few thoughts, don't you think? Before you get all anxious and think you've bought a book written by a crazy, god worshipping anti-vax person, relax, you haven't. The big pharmaceutical companies have done so much for all of us – in fact, vaccinations are probably one of the best examples of how big pharma (and science obviously) have changed lives for the better.

I'm not suggesting we abandon what is working. The aim of this book is to encourage us to stop doing what has made great things bad. We are popping anti-depressants like it is candy these days. We hide our pain instead of voicing it. Those are good things that have gone wrong. And we can change it – by going back to kindness. The kinder we treat ourselves, the kinder we will treat others and that way, we will change the world for the better – one kind act at a time.

Let's do this.

Another important area where a lack of kindness is causing a lot of pain is mental health and how we respond to it. Anything to do with mental health is looked at with contempt and disgust. 'Nurturing Kindness' wants to change that. In this book, we'll look at different mental health challenges and how to manage them healthily and sustainably. We also look at what causes us to cover up our mental health struggles and learn how kindness is a key player in feeling better.

It is important to point out that this book is NOT intended to try and replace your healthcare professionals. You DO need to keep seeing your counsellor, or your psychiatrist if they are part of your healthcare team. This book does not give any medical advice in any way. Please see your doctor if you would like to discuss concerns or questions regarding medication that can help you manage your mental health.

My book, 'Nurturing Kindness', should be seen as additional support to what you have in place to help you live your life in the best way you want.

Most importantly, I want you to use this book to help you feel better so you can keep doing YOU – because that is what you do best!

Introduction

Kindness lives in our hearts, souls and minds. It blossoms where we are most vulnerable and raw as humans. That's where its strength lies and is also its challenge in today's time. So many of us are not well mentally, and thanks to the shady manipulators, we have been led to believe that being mentally unwell is bad, icky and something to be ashamed of. As a result, we talk about mental health but don't understand it fully.

I get it. Mental health is complex and that makes it scary, physical health can also be scary. We are told that it is normal and absolutely okay to be physically sick, have broken bones or an open, bleeding wound. That kind of stuff we can see, taste, smell and experience it out in the open. That makes it less scary because we can process it on a rather primitive level. Mental health on the other hand – it is invisible.

You can't tell by just looking at someone if they are mentally well or not. Chances are that you are working with someone who is dealing with a major mental health challenge, but you don't know it. Such is the struggle of anyone living with an invisible illness or disability. Their suffering is overlooked because there is no open, bleeding wound people can gawk at. Their pain is nonetheless real and deserves attention and healing.

It is a fact that mental health needs to be important to all of us. We talk about self-care, especially for women, but hardly ever mention that we need to look after our mind and soul. We often think of a spa day or pedicure as self-care, but therapy is rarely thought of as something to include in the way we look after ourselves!

Those of us who struggle and feel overwhelmed feel pressured into staying quiet about our challenges. We know deep down that our mental health needs to come first if we want to feel better. We know that self-care is not light and fluffy and can be scary and challenging at times. Instead of being encouraged to explore our mental health and give it time and attention, we are often 'encouraged' to keep quiet about it. This can make us feel dirty or that attending to our mental health is not important.

So, it should come as no surprise that the number of people experiencing mental health problems keeps rising. The consequences of undiagnosed conditions are highly concerning, and we are not well enough prepared to address the crisis the mental health sector is experiencing all around the country. The need for support and treatment is high; the funding, facilities and necessary staff are low. This presents sufferers with many challenges. It is hard to get the right help. People get passed on from one healthcare professional to another and often end up with a script for medication but no real help and support.

Mental health is complex, and it takes time to find the best treatment plan and support. This stands in stark contrast to a healthcare system (and society as a whole) that is always under pressure to perform to the highest standard without the necessary equipment and manpower in place. The dark consequences of that can no longer be ignored – those who are most vulnerable and in crisis often don't even bother to reach out for help due to negative experiences. As a result, they end up suffering in silence. That is NOT ok. It is NOT acceptable. We cannot continue to silence those whose voice is already weak from the daily struggle that is mental illness.

As mentioned in the welcome note, this book does not give any medical advice. That still must be sought from healthcare professionals. This book is a manifesto for those who feel voiceless at times. You don't have to suffer in silence anymore. Take this book with you; use it for comfort and encouragement. Let it help you find your voice in situations where it is hard to speak.

Kindness has taken such a beating that it seems it has disappeared from the world of medicine and mental health as a whole. Being kind to someone who is mentally unwell almost seems like a dangerous act because anyone being kind to those struggling seems to take a risk being associated with 'those people'. And none of the cool kids would accept that. So, we don't help, we are not kind, we are not caring, just so we can fit in. But - kindness DOES fit in; it breaks barriers, changes perceptions and challenges us to look closer, deeper and with more love. That is why mental health needs a huge amount of kindness each and every day so it can grow.

Of course, we don't always have to use words to find our own way of living kindly – sometimes actions speak louder than words. That is especially true when dealing with mental illness. Taking time to properly address anxiety or depression is a powerful thing to do. It is time to stop being silenced by others and their expectations about our wellbeing. Many changes can be made within our own four walls and it can be the place from where we keep building.

That is why self-care is so crucial. Good self-care must include taking care of your mental health. This will help you to be in a good place to deal with anything else that happens in your life. Self-care isn't always pretty. It is not about fancy, sparkly nails but sitting with your pain instead. This means that for effective self-care, we need to give room to those thoughts that want us to believe we are not good enough.

Thoughts like 'I'd be better off dead,!' – 'No one will miss me.' Or 'I am such a failure because (insert reason).' Such thoughts are dark and certainly not pretty. But the moment we acknowledge them, they start to lose their power. THAT is self-care, too. And sometimes it is learning the best technique and strategy to tackle an anxiety attack or to admit that today, getting out of bed is the only task ticked off your to-do list.

Shame

A sneaky bitch

Before we dive into different techniques and dos and don'ts's for looking after our mental health, we need to nip one thing in the bud straight away and address how it impacts on our mental wellbeing:

Don't compare your struggles to others.

Comparing ourselves to others is a total buzz kill in most life situations. It takes the joy out of happy moments and throws darkness on already difficult moments. No healing can be done if we compare our challenges and our healing progress to others. This will simply put unnecessary doubts into your mind, negate any progress you have made and give you the feeling of failure. Comparison opens the door to complicated feelings such as shame and leads to loss of self-worth faster than you can say stop.

Shame is quite a tricky bitch and one that deserves our attention if we want to better understand good mental health care. Of course, there are a few components that contribute to feeling well mentally but shame is certainly one of the big players. It can be hidden, and we are often not even aware it is the underlying cause of our challenges and upsets. Often, shame masks itself as depression as some of the signs are similar. Many people don't realize that shame is the trigger for feeling terrible or even anxious. It is worth your time and highly beneficial for your healing to dive deeper into shame and what it is all about. You might be surprised what you will find.

Shame has usually been with us from childhood. Not necessarily consciously, but it takes place in our being right from our early days. You see, shame has long been used as a tool to raise children. We get shamed into doing things or behaving in a way our parents want us to. Think of the moment you were forced to sit at the table and weren't allowed to leave until you finished everything, even if it was disgusting Brussels sprouts (or some other food that you didn't like the taste of) on the plate. You may have been shamed for having the audacity to say no to something that was given to you. Instead of validating your taste buds, you were shamed for having them.

Children were often made to feel bad so they could 'learn' what was right. Many parents probably didn't think twice about applying those strategies and for a long time, their kids appeared to be fine. These parents are also often surprised when their adolescent or adult child struggles with depression and anxiety (for real this time).

The thing with shame is that it devalues you instantly. Nothing matters anymore once shame takes over. One word can be enough and causes shame to come flooding back. It can lie dormant in many of us for ages but resurfaces more often in people who live with depression and anxiety. This is why I want to address shame here.

Take a moment and look at your life so far. Have you been raised using shame to get you to behave? Do you feel shame is part of your struggle (such as feeling ashamed because you can't get up – again)? Are you aware that shame is part of your challenge?

If you haven't been aware – that is 100% FINE.

Shame works like that. It doesn't need big recognition to do its work. In fact, it works better and more effectively if we don't know it is there. It is a sneaky bitch for sure. It lurks in the shadows of our being, waiting to pounce. So, it is absolutely okay if you are only becoming aware of shame in your story now.

There is research into shame done by the wonderful and exceptional Dr Brené Brown who tell us that shame needs three things 'to grow exponentially in our lives: secrecy, silence and judgment'.

If you are only now becoming aware that shame has indeed been part of your path as you read this, it is quite likely because nobody around you talks about shame or having used it on you. I doubt any parent would openly admit that they shamed their kids into behaving while thinking they were doing the right thing. That's secrecy and silence right there. On the other hand, if you are like me and have found yourself living life outside of the box and getting judged for it, you have quite possibly felt devalued, useless and a failure because of that judgment. That is shame working at its best.

Shame - a sneaky bitch. I am dedicating this space to shame because I believe it is essential to acknowledge and work with it to be successful at managing or even overcoming depression and anxiety.

This doesn't mean in any way, that people struggling with anxiety and depression are the only ones experiencing shame. Nope. We ALL live with shame and shame runs deep. This is a simple fact. Let's be straight here – this is not a blame (shame) fest. It's about becoming more aware of where our problems and challenges are rooted in. Shame can be a very powerful breeding ground for anxiety and depression. Another one is trauma. It is very hard to separate shame from trauma. We will learn more about trauma and shame later. We all want to know how we can feel better. Knowing and revisiting our experiences with shame is one way to do that.

Of course, the next question must be – what can we do to deal with shame?

I quote once more the amazing Brené Brown, who teaches us that 'empathy is the antidote to shame'. I would like to add 'kindness' to this. Empathy and kindness go together well and work their magic best when used at the same time. It is not always easy to do. Have you ever had someone tell you to be gentle with yourself, told you to take it easy or go slow? Often, that is great advice; but are we allowing ourselves to do it? In most cases, we don't. We would really want our friends to do it and believe they absolutely deserve it, but for ourselves, not so much. We can be kind to others but don't allow ourselves the kindness we deserve.

We can't seem to pull off the one thing that will stop shame dead in its tracks - we struggle to be emphatic and kind with ourselves. We haven't been taught to do it. Women tend to be way too hard on themselves. The thought of not being good enough the way they are is stuck to them like bad smells in a male public restroom. It seems impenetrable.

We do have the solution to shame, but it is up to us to apply it. Shame can't survive empathy and kindness. Empathy and kindness have their roots in love – shame does not. Love can overcome anything – shame cannot.

Let's look at a few ways you can practice kindness and empathy. As you go along and become more experienced in living with kindness, you will find that shame will diminish.

Be gentle

Didn't we just hear that? Indeed, we have. I am putting it on my advice list for the following reasons - It is the right thing to do. Are you someone who thinks harshly of yourself? What are the words that come to mind if you didn't accomplish something? Do useless, hopeless, failure, disgusting, loser and the like sound familiar? If you answered yes, then you are certainly not alone. That is the harsh judgment (and one thriving factor of shame) I mentioned before. It is often second nature for many of us.

Try the gentle approach instead. Maybe you didn't clean the oven, the dishes and the floors today. That's okay. Tell yourself you did great. You ticked a few things off the to do list. Be gentle and allow yourself to focus on the positive side of things – the things you finished off. Allow yourself to feel enough for what you have done, and sometimes, that might have just been getting out of bed.

Be patient

Shame is not in a hurry. It feels very safe lurking about, and it becomes quite comfortable when left to stay where it is. It is really important that we allow time to apply empathy to erase shame. Empathy is very powerful, and it will do its magic – as long as we allow it in. It can feel strange at first to be gentle with ourselves, and to push shame aside. We are not used to it. The key is practice. Reverting back into harsh judgment of ourselves is common. After all, it has probably been a habit for many years. It might even be the first time you have truly tried showing kindness towards yourself. If you find it hard to be gentle, cut yourself some slack and allow what is, instead of what you think should be - it's okay. You can always try again. Be okay with small progress steps.

Focus on yourself

This is your story, your journey. We all experience shame differently so don't compare and don't be apologetic about the way you are weeding out yours. Don't explain yourself to those who don't understand. Healing takes energy, don't waste yours on trying to explain or making others more aware. Right now, it is about you. Allow yourself to shift the focus to yourself and your wellbeing.

This is not always easy. As women, we are nurturers and that is a great thing. It is also something that is being exploited in our patriarchal society where it is seen as a given and something everybody can and should take advantage of. I mean, is it a coincidence that the job of being a mother is the hardest there is yet is recognized so little (not to mention the lack of pay)? Don't feel bad if you find it hard to put your needs first. It is awkward for many of us to do just that.

Start small

Spend a certain amount of time on your story and explore where you shame is coming from. Then stop and move away from it. You're setting the pace. Do make time in your calendar to focus on yourself and make room to practice empathy and killing of shame. It is me time. It might not feel like it when you first start because it is uncomfortable, but you will start to heal and grow and come to treasure the fact that you made yourself a priority.

Listen to yourself

In today's world where there is so much chatter, and every person seems to know just the thing for you, it has become difficult to tune out and listen inwardly. What does your mind tell you about your shame in a quiet moment? It can be frightening at first to confront ourselves. It makes us vulnerable as we lay bare what we have hidden away for so long, but that's okay. Empathy needs to go to those darker layers of our being to usurp shame.

We need to meet our shame as it is – raw, uncomfortable, and ugly. What does that mean in a practical sense? When I say listen to yourself, I mean pay attention to the reactions you experience when you think about shame or where it might come from. Do you get hot and flustered? Do you feel sad and defeated and suddenly drained? Whatever it is you feel – it is okay. Just take note. Don't judge it, don't overthink it. Use these emotions as a guideline. As we work on our shame and it diminishes, those feelings will fade away. The weaker they get, the more progress you are making. Once again, you set the pace. Don't try and rush and don't feel bad if you struggle. This is not easy work! You will get there in our own time and that is the only thing that matters.

A word needs to be said here about ever being free of shame. That is not likely to happen. Shame is a built-in emotion like anger or joy. There is such a thing as healthy shame as wise people have called it. Healthy shame is a useful tool that can guide us towards appropriate behaviour in different situations – such as not taking our pants off in the middle of an important business meeting. That does not mean healthy shame is great to experience – who likes to blush, slump their shoulders and just wish they could disappear into thin air? It is an emotion that we can't and should not try to get rid of. Used properly, shame can teach us important lessons that will stick because of the way it made us feel. Shame is hard to forget as it lurks everywhere in our body, makes our stomach lurch, and causes us to avert our eyes or can stop us dead in our tracks because of a certain memory.

The trick is to learn from the lesson and move forward. Shame becomes unhealthy when it triggers us to think we are inadequate or stupid for saying something silly at a party. The moment we start to dwell on situations and start fretting about what other people might have thought, shame is no longer healthy. Once it attacks our self-worth, it has become toxic. Shame can be a useful tool, but it needs tight reigns. We don't want it to allow judgment, secrecy and silence to rock up and take over the scene. Shame has its place but that's all it is entitled to – a place in our range of emotions, it should never be the driving factor for actions, thoughts and emotions. It is not a king at the table; it is merely a guest.

Of course, putting shame into its place is not always easy. As we start to examine it and explore the impact shame has left on our journeys, it can be quite shocking to realise just how often it has been used on us, or how many times we have used it ourselves because we thought it was the best option. Dealing, acknowledging and cataloguing shame will take time.

First, we need to remember how shame presents itself; it often appears in the form of humiliation, shyness or embarrassment. That is exactly why shame is such a tricky bitch! Something happens and we think, feel or say 'Oh, I'm so embarrassed!'. In reality, we are likely to be feeling shame. It can be hard to put our finger on a situation and realise that we experienced shame and not embarrassment or an unexpected bout of shyness. We might feel icky and deeply unsettled, wondering why we feel so terrible about an embarrassing moment. It was just a slip up after all! Yes, it was, it was also shame jumping at its chance to spread through our body.

Shame can rip open old wounds we thought had long healed. It normally pops up when we were expecting a positive reaction but get a negative one instead, or when we have tried to make a connection only to find ourselves being rejected. Feeling ashamed is an indication of our needs not being met - especially our emotional needs. It can leave us feeling bad for having them in the first place - as if we're not deserving. It is important to learn that there is nothing wrong with wanting our needs met. Shame tells us we're being silly for wanting our mother's attention to show off our latest tricks. Shame is great at making sure the feeling of rejection goes deep, and this often causes it to stick with us well into our adult years. Needless to say, that kind of shame is far from healthy.

There are steps that you can and should take to heal from toxic shame.

Shame thrives on us feeling unworthy and like a failure. But what lies underneath those negative emotions? It's simple – our basic human needs. We want connection with others, we want to be part of our family or community, we want to feel and know that we BELONG.

Wanting to belong is perfectly natural and is important to fulfil your needs, longings, hopes and dreams. Remind yourself that you deserve to have them fulfilled! Tell yourself that you are worthy of having your needs met! By doing that, you push shame right back into its place. Be gentle with yourself though and give yourself time. It might be easier to dismiss your needs, to try and ignore them or even to tell yourself you don't deserve to have your needs met. That is the way we are conditioned, especially women. It is NOT right to deny yourself these much-needed connections. Looking after yourself means more than just having a regular spa day; you also need to go deeper into your emotions and allow yourself to feel grounded within and to do so without feeling shame for spending time on yourself.

When we talk about connection, we're referring to relationships that are healing, helpful and enriching for us. For us to thrive as human beings, we need to surround ourselves with people who are ready to celebrate us the way we are and who are glad to have us in their lives. We need people who know that we are enough the way we are. Shame has no place in a circle that is supportive and encourages us to claim our rightful spot in life.

Lastly, we need to be aware that some rejection and setbacks in life are inevitable. We can't let that stop us from getting out there to look for connections. We have to stop being afraid to be vulnerable to others in our quest to find love and belonging. This doesn't mean we have to do what we think others want us to do – not at all. We need to take a leap of faith now and then, take a chance and see what happens. The outcome being unpredictable shouldn't stop us and fear of rejection should never hinder us from trying to get what we want. If we don't dare to be brave, shame has won.

I'm not suggesting anyone should jump into something new at every opportunity. We don't have to do something outside of our comfort zone every day. There are times when we simply need to take a step back and think things through before acting. We won't heal from shame effectively by putting ourselves out there day after day without a break. Take that leap of faith when something really important is involved – like mending a valuable relationship or having a go at a job we're not formally trained for, but know we'll be great at. In those moments, we need to tell shame to bugger off, dare to be brave and give it our best shot. It might not be easy, but it will be rewarding, worthwhile and healing.

Belonging

In the previous chapter, we touched briefly on our deep need to belong. I want to dedicate more time to this now as it is so essential for our wellbeing, our healing and our ability to have unlimited kindness. We thrive through our relationships. We can clearly see this in newborns as they depend on their mother to survive, grow and learn. If a newborn is not exposed to human interaction, they don't develop properly. Connection to other human beings is the most important driving force for a good start to life.

A sense of belonging comes from connecting to people we care about, and who care for us. When we feel safe in our relationships, we know where we belong. This sounds really simple, and in many ways it is. At the same time, this is where our biggest stepping-stone lies. As soon as we find ourselves without any connections, or the ones we do have are unhealthy, trauma develops.

Another factor that shouldn't be underestimated when it comes to belonging is our environment. Many external influences have a deep impact on our ability to know where we belong. When people are uprooted from their home due to war, natural disasters or other tragedies, they experience the loss of belonging on a very deep and traumatic level. As it is with human tragedy, trauma doesn't discriminate. Children that grow up in violent homes struggle to belong and continue to do so as adults. Kids who have to move around a lot when they are growing up often feel lost and like they don't belong anywhere. The trauma of not belonging is all around us. With it comes different challenges.

The question 'where do I belong?' is not easily answered, but that's not the point. The point is that it CAN be answered, and your own personal answer might surprise you. To find it, you will need patience, courage and kindness. It will require looking back on your life to establish where the connection was lost or fractured. Has it never really been there, or did it break off at a certain stage during childhood? This can be a painful process; it can be very unpleasant to dive deep and establish where this feeling of not belonging comes from. It is important to point out here; this is a situation where we have short-term pain for long-term gain. Think about this nagging feeling of knowing that something is amiss. Isn't it just incredibly irritating and draining? Does it cause you anxiety or depression?

If you said yes to these questions, you're ready to address this challenge. This suggests that you know something needs to change to feel better and be at ease with who you are, and where you belong. These thoughts and feelings serve as a reminder that work needs to be done; but more importantly, you are aware of it. You can do this! You have completed the first step towards healing, which is becoming aware that an area in your life needs your attention. This may cause you to think you've failed because there are a few things to figure out; that is NOT true. Living life means experiencing constant change and growth. We should address our challenges as they come along. Some will come back to us in different forms because they have very important lessons for us and let's face it, we don't always learn the first time around. That's all that is. Nurturing Kindness and being consciously aware of our learning process in life is the best way to go forward. Knowing where you belong IS a big lesson and kindness applied to yourself will help you along the way.

So, let's get to it and take the first step.

Where do you belong?

Think about what brings you joy. What makes your heart sing? Is it an activity, a place or people? Is it a combination of the three? Or is it a state of mind? We often think that belonging is attached to our upbringing. In cases where a happy family nurtured and protected a child, that is certainly true. In this instance, belonging can mean 'I belong with my family'. That's fantastic but it is not the be-all and end-all. Belonging is way more than that and that's where its strength lies. YOU get to decide. You can leave social conditioning behind and define what belonging means for you. It does NOT need to be attached to your family. If you feel you don't belong to your parents or caregivers anymore (or have never felt that way) that is perfectly fine.

The importance of belonging lies in that we claim it for ourselves in a way that suits us. We should not allow other people to dictate what makes us happy. If you go to the beach or forest and feel happy, grounded and at peace there, that is a place where you belong. If that feeling comes more from being at a table with good friends, you belong there. If you get lost in writing or painting, that's your place of belonging. If you find fulfilment in travelling to a new destination, then that is where you belong.

Belonging does NOT have to be hard. That's the thing about it. It requires our awareness and courage to make it our own and stop listening to the old-fashioned and very outdated notions of belonging. 'A wife belongs to her husband', 'a mother belongs to her family', and 'a woman belongs in the kitchen'. NOPE. You belong where you CHOOSE to belong. Once you find it, stick with it, treasure it, be proud of it and OWN it. Don't let others tell you what is right or wrong. You know your heart and soul best and where it will find lasting, empowering and healthy joy and fulfilment.

We need to move away from the notion that belonging comes with sacrifice or is complicated. We make it complicated. I am often reminded of a particular young person I met; I immediately thought, 'this person is utterly and completely lost and doesn't know where they belong'. It shocked me when that thought popped up, especially as the person knew something was wrong but couldn't put their finger on it. Being young is challenging; it is difficult being a teenager about to enter adulthood! Feeling lost and unsure at that age comes with the territory, but it was more than that. This person was told by the people around them that something was wrong with them because they were always depressed. And that looking after your mental health meant going to therapy.

This put me in an awkward position because being a therapist myself, I agree that going to therapy can be and IS highly beneficial for good mental health care. But not always and certainly not in this case. I strongly felt that this young person needed to feel a sense of belonging. They were so restricted by their own environment that there was hardly any room to breathe. If we are so caged in by outside expectations, knowing where we belong is made extra hard when it doesn't have to be.

Knowing where we belong can take time, and that is okay. As a culture, we need to have more trust and kindness available to all who seek it. Let them decide where they know and feel they belong and let's move obstacles (aka our own perceptions and conditioning of belonging) out of the way for them. For parents, it is super scary to see our children so lost. It is taxing for us as friends and relatives to watch someone struggle to find their place. It is often very emotional, and it fucking sucks. But if we remove our expectations about belonging, we could help a lot of people. Just ease up on the assumption that young people must know all about their life at the tender age of 18. Take a step back from expecting women to have everything figure out and that they can do things with ease because they 'belong' in a role assigned to them by a patriarchal society. Smash the cages our thoughts and feelings are trapped in and explore where you belong!

When we know where we belong, a lot of things fall in place. Life becomes easier and more manageable. We feel at peace which is wonderful and so important. As always in life, change is inevitable. Don't be afraid if you suddenly feel like you no longer belong where you once did; this can change over a lifetime to suit our current circumstances, and that is absolutely fine.

Let's talk about two things here. It is absolutely fine when you find you belong WITH people or a specific person. A wife can belong with her husband and vice versa, a wife can belong with a wife, a husband with a husband. Absolutely! When two soul mates meet then you belong together. In this union, you have the best foundation to grow and nurture kindness. Simples.

As I mentioned earlier, we need to ignore the old-fashioned notion of a wife belonging to her husband'; we need to change the perception of one human belonging TO another. Saying 'a wife belongs to her husband' has caused a great deal of domestic violence to go unnoticed. Women and children suffering at the hands of violent men because she is supposed to stay with him, she belongs TO him. Umm, no! That is NOT healthy and needs to stop. If you find that one special person who really sees you for you, cherishes your heart and soul then hell yeah, you belong together! When we define our belonging with another person, all we need to know is that it is for the better, not for worse. We will stay with them in sickness and in health but we ain't putting up with toxic shit that doesn't sustain, support or empower us.

Belonging 'with' someone doesn't only include our love interests; it also refers to family and friends. All we need is the freedom to make that choice that rings true in our hearts. A choice that not only enriches our lives but those who are close to us as well. At the heart of belonging is our need for human connection. It is what we seek and what helps us thrive and grow. A deep and meaningful connection to others is incredibly healing and powerful. In a world where we tend to isolate ourselves more and more, this need becomes more apparent again. It's lovely to have nice things, but in our very core, we want to experience that sense of belonging and know that we matter to someone. That is why it pays to dedicate the time needed to find where you belong and who with. Do it over and over again where needed. We need it and most certainly deserve it!

Another word needs to be said about trauma as the reason for not belonging. The world we live in can often be a nasty place. Not many people are born privileged, not everyone starts life in a safe and nourishing environment. An environment where a sense of belonging either comes easy and naturally; or where we at least have enough self-confidence to venture out and find our own true place of belonging. For some, life is rough from the beginning. When life starts with trauma, it often continues on that path. Not only will people feel lost, they actually are lost. They end up in situations they never wanted to be in. The pain of not feeling wanted, loved or appreciated can be overbearing and can intensify the feeling of not belonging tenfold.

Add violence and/or struggles with an addiction to the mix and life becomes survival, not enjoyment. This kind of search to belong and feel that we are wanted is a whole new level of challenge. It is not up to us to say what is possible and what is not. The most important thing for us is to keep seeing the person in their uniqueness instead of their problem, addiction or struggle. We must see and recognize their pain and stop judging. A place to belong is something we all want and for some, this journey takes them to dark, dark corners of life. We can't map out the way for them, but we can help by focusing on who they are and not on who we think they are. The road to belonging for anyone needs to be paved with kindness, not good intentions, assumptions and a fuck ton of judgment.

You are Enough

When it comes to finding our true place of belonging, it goes hand in hand with knowing that we are enough. We seem to have lost sight of that in a world where we are constantly pushed to be better, fitter, healthier and apparently entirely different than who we are now. Kindness towards ourselves has become rare. It's as if being enough is admitting that we gave up because we must never allow ourselves to be content!

Of course, there is nothing wrong with wanting to improve ourselves! The issue is deeper than that. It's the notion that we are not good enough to start with; and MUST change to make us lovable, acceptable, and reputable. This puts so much pressure on anyone who is struggling with mental health issues, body image, self-worth and self-love. Finding something about ourselves we can improve should never make us feel ashamed of who we are. If that is the case, you're looking at self-improvement the wrong way. It is always great to try and live healthier, to go back to school to learn new skills or to start healing from past trauma. That is good for you, empowering and another step in your journey. We can always take those actions and feel good about it! If you are doing this then you have welcomed kindness back into your personal life. You are looking at yourself lovingly and not through harsh and unforgiving lenses some people seem to expect us to use.

More often than not, the thought of not being good enough comes easier than thinking we are. But we ARE good enough! Struggling with mental health does not mean you are not good enough. It just is what it is. You are enough the way you are – with or without mental health struggles. The challenges you were given do not impact on your self-worth. They are part of you but don't define you. It is hard to remember that when we are surrounded by constant advertising about this shake or that drink that will help us stay or become thin. This creates the misconception that only when we are skinny, we are going to be accepted by others. We can forget we are good enough when social media blasts us with happy pics of people who seem to have it all; they always appear to be in control and never have a bad day. Most of that is utter bullshit, yet it is out there and for all of us who are sensitive, insecure and simply struggle to get through certain days; it makes us feel so unworthy.

That is where we need to stop! You are enough. Right now, right as you are now.

Did you struggle to get out of bed today?
You are enough.

Haven't washed your hair in a week?
You are enough.

Have you struggled to leave the house today because of anxiety, depression or both?
You are enough.

Are you carrying extra weight?
You are enough.

YOU ARE ENOUGH

We need to change how we look at our lives, our achievements or failures and cut out the judgment entirely. Especially as women, we are our harshest critics and we often start with a bad thing when we talk about ourselves. We describe ourselves with negative adjectives instead of positives. We have been conditioned from our early days to believe we are not supposed to love ourselves and be proud of what we can do. Instead, we are often told to be quiet; not to be proud of our talents and for the love of God - please fit in!! Be obedient not a rebel. Be fucking quiet and don't raise hell. Whenever we don't play along, we get shamed instantly. So of course, we start to feel that we are not good enough. Being loud is often deemed to be undesirable for girls so, as grown women we then feel bad when we do speak up to question things and demand answers. We might know instinctively when we really need to do so; but when the reaction we get from others makes us feel like a nuisance, we may start to think we are not good enough. Do we then remain quiet because that is what is expected of us?

Fuck that!

YOU ARE ENOUGH

You are enough, especially when you speak up; because you defy the expectations of others and are not quiet when there is something that needs to be questioned!!!

You need to do YOU. And you **ARE** enough!

If you think this is a bit repetitive, you would be right; it needs to be.

We are so used to hearing what we are doing wrong and what is undesirable about ourselves, our appearance, ambitions and our hopes and dreams. We end up chasing a version of ourselves that feels entirely wrong to our heart and soul, but we do it anyway. We don't get nearly enough messages that tell us that we are enough. So, let's start now.

You are enough.

You are beautiful.

You are unique.

You matter.

Right now, right here, the way you are.

We are imperfectly perfect, and that's the way we should be. The first step to healing has been taken. Keep going. **You've got this!**

When we change how we look at and talk about ourselves, we feel better and start to heal. We also open ourselves up for genuine kindness to take hold in our hearts, souls and minds. It will become normal, and kindness will always reside within you, helping you to be you. Some people talk about your light and letting it shine, I believe kindness is the force that ignites it and keeps it burning strong. When we are kind to ourselves, and it has become a habit, it kind of recycles itself. It feeds itself and keeps you strong. All we need to do is change our mindset, allow ourselves to turn things upside down and change it all for the better.

Depression

"Pain is real. But so is hope."
Unknown

There is much talk about how you can 'heal' yourself from mental illness. That can be a dangerous line to walk because it implies that mental illness is a bad thing to have when it is not; it is what it is. It can be managed. Mental health is part of us, just like physical health and there is nothing wrong with it.

That is not to say experiencing depression isn't challenging, it is. But we need to see it for what it is – a challenge. It is not a life sentence; it's not the end of the road.

The first step to feeling better is to truly realise that we are not 'damaged goods' because we suffer from depression. You are NOT damaged; you are unwell and temporarily so. It is very irritating to know that people have been conditioned to think mental illness is something to be ashamed of. We are not ashamed if we have a cold or the flu! Let's extend that and STOP being ashamed of having depression or anxiety.

The second step to feeling better is to be kind to yourself. Yes, once more it comes down to kindness, and to apply it first to ourselves so we can then carry it out to the world to help others.

As we have established in previous chapters, women especially can be unkind to themselves. They often feel like they don't deserve it. They are kind and caring towards everyone else but not to themselves. And when we get hit with a diagnosis like depression or anxiety, we definitely don't consider taking a breath and slowing down. No, we are most likely upset and feel like a failure because now we have 'that', too. The truth is – you are not a failure. And you deserve to be kind to yourself. In fact, it is imperative!

When we start being kind to ourselves, we are better able to extend that kindness to others. And by doing that, we can help them understand what it is like to live with something like depression, anxiety or any invisible illness. Kindness is the spark to all healing – our own as well as that of others. So, allow yourself to be kind. This can come in many forms, and there is no one size fits all kind of approach to it. Kindness can be getting a haircut even if it's not exactly in this week's budget. Being kind to yourself can be acknowledging that you managed to brush your hair today, or realising you need help from others. Kindness is looking at your actions without any judgment. It means looking at yourself gently. Depression is a tough motherfucker to deal with. Some days that means we have to take it slowly and that is okay. We need to be unapologetic in our approach to mental health. It is not about what others think we should do; it is about doing what is best for us. It is also about not beating ourselves up for reaching our limit for the day.

Too many of the young women I see in my practice tell me what failures they are because they struggle in social situations; or because they find it hard to keep a job. My dear young soul – you are NOT a failure. You are amazing just the way you are. We need to stop being so incredibly tough on ourselves. It is okay to struggle in social situations. Occasions we would normally be happy and bubbly at but find we only feel darkness inside are not easy; these are not good for our mental health. Instead of feeling like a failure, be proud of yourself for recognizing that certain situations are not good for you at this time. That is your strength shining through.

Keeping a job can be challenging at the best of times, and it doesn't get any easier with a mental health issue in tow. If you're managing to get out of bed and go to work every day, be proud of that achievement. I know it is not always that straightforward. Not everyone understands the struggle of depression just yet. If you have lost a job before due to your health, know that it was a toxic place for you to be at in the first place. I know that doesn't pay the bills; but by being true to yourself and your needs, you will find a way that is healthier for you. You can do this. In fact, you are already doing this by showing up every day for life and its challenges. That deserves a fucking medal, and a whole lot of kindness showered upon you by yourself. You are tougher than you think, and you are doing well. Remember that and say it out loud when the other nagging and negative voices creep up on you again. They need to take a very long break away from you and your mental health.

We have covered the important basics of dealing with depression – knowing you are not damaged in any way, and that you need to be kind to yourself to start healing. We can now look at a few practical things you can do in everyday life to ward off the darkness. The challenge is to make sure you don't give in. Let's look at a few ways this can be done.

First up, we cover the absolute no-nos. It's important to know these, as the main struggle seems to be the pressure from outside that expects us to be ready to perform at 100% all of the time. By rejecting those expectations, we are on our way to feeling better already. Do remember these following points! This is not an absolute list and you should feel free to add your own don'ts to the list. I have left some blank space for you to add your own. It is about starting your healing process and you not only need to do what works for you best, but it is imperative you do it. It is YOUR mental wellbeing we are talking about!!!

DON'T:

- Be hard on yourself
- Think you are weak
- Blame yourself
- Put pressure on yourself to feel better
- Feel bad if you cry
- Apologise for taking time to recover

Look at the list on the previous page and take some time to reflect. Have you done any of these things? Have you thought of your depression as a weakness? Have you pressured yourself to think you should feel better? If you answered yes, that is absolutely fine. We all do it. After all, it is so easy to blame ourselves and to perceive our struggle as something 'bad'. The simple truth is though – it is not. This can't be said enough!

The importance of our mental health should never be underestimated. It is very much part of us, just like our physical health. It deserves time and daily attention - aka kindness, applied to ourselves. Of course, we are not used to giving our mental wellbeing that kind of room in our lives, and when it goes downhill, we feel bad, weak and guilty. That is where our old foe shame comes in strongly. It feeds on our vulnerability and insecurities and obviously loves the fact that we are conditioned to think of mental health as something yucky and undesirable. Shame always lurks in the shadows, and we have been told that mental health belongs there, too. It does not.

Mental health and taking care of it belongs out in the open, always. We need to stop apologizing, not only for making mental health a priority but also for our struggles with it. It is time to stop suffering in silence. As we know from talking about shame, it thrives on secrecy and loneliness. Feeling like we can't and shouldn't talk about mental health is detrimental to our wellbeing, but no need to blame ourselves. We already know we feel lonely and pressured into being silent because our struggles might make others feel uncomfortable. Therefore, it has become second nature to try and feel better instantly, or to apologise because we can't seem to get better. We can be very harsh in the way we talk about ourselves because of the vibes we get from the outside world; a world that often does not want to concern itself with mental health. This has to stop!

Your focus needs to be on YOUR mental health, don't worry about how other people perceive it. YOU can change how you think and feel about your mental health. YOU have the power to stop thinking about your mental health as something negative. It will take time; we are so used to living with these negative perceptions, and it can be hard to let go of them. This is not a competition, and it's not about who gets to change their mindset first. This is all about you, and you set the pace to suit yourself, there is no need to rush. You will have great successes and breakthroughs and maybe some setbacks. It's all part of the journey.

It's a good idea to start small and then build up. A nice way to start changing the way you perceive your mental health is to remind yourself that it is part of us. Tell yourself how awesome, amazing and fabulous you are for looking after it. Of course, when we are stuck in the claws of depression, it can feel impossible to tell ourselves how wonderful we are.

That's okay. Here's what you can do instead.

- Leave your day free of things you 'must' do
- The day, the hour, the minute you are in – it is what it is
- Don't focus on what you 'should' do – just think about the next step to get through the day

- Rest up – for long stances if you can or lots of short rests, depending on your situation
- Do nothing

You can take care of your mental health by simply listening to what your mind and body tell you. If it is too hard to get out of bed, don't do it. We live in a busy world where people sometimes get dirty looks for daring to take their 30-minute lunch break! When you are in the midst of depression, resting and taking a break is essential to healing. You are often exhausted and feel drained. You need to rest!

I am fully aware we are always walking a fine line with depression. Too much resting can lead to complete surrender to depression. Even if we find ourselves going down that path, feeling ashamed is certainly not going to help us get better. We must stop thinking that a little bit of depression is okay but not too much! Please, keep that away from me! The fact is many people struggle with depression; and for some, this struggle can become too exhausting, too overwhelming and just too much. They can't fight alone and the best thing we can do, either as friends or as a society, is to be understanding and free of judgment.

Psychiatric wards have been created to help people get better. They are NOT an invitation for random people to have an opinion about others who seek help there. A lot of people are okay walking to a doctor's office or the emergency room because of a broken bone or a physical illness. The same standard should be possible for people who seek help for mental health issues. We should all be able to walk into any situation, any doctor's office or emergency room and be received with kindness and lack of judgment from others, just like the guy who broke his nose playing footy.

Let's come back to you and how to practice changing your perception of mental health. Remember it is okay to just get through the day sometimes. Hour by hour, minute by minute where necessary. It's also okay to fall back to old thinking about mental health; you can try anew tomorrow. Small steps do the trick. The change will be lasting if we start with one thing rather than a million. So, leave any unrealistic expectations about yourself or how you are supposed to feel and be out of your head.

Always, always remember, this is not a competition! The goal is for YOU to feel better and more hopeful, and you **will** get there in your own time. It does NOT matter when that is or if your friend feels better before you do.

After the don'ts now let's look at things you **can do**. Feel free to add some positive actions in the space below.

DO:

- Allow yourself to not be ok
- Take your time to improve
- Express your feelings in a safe way
- Create strategies that are right for YOU
- Seek support
- Retreat to recharge

When our mental health is not good, everything is out of whack. Physical health will suffer and then suddenly, it is all downhill from there. That is why we do need to take time out and evaluate what we can do to feel better. The strategies you choose might change over time or you may even find something that always works for you. Here are a few suggestions. You can add to this list in the blank space below if you wish.

- Paint, draw, doodle
- Write
- Create with different fabrics and tools
- Go outside and soak up some sun – all seasons
- Gentle exercise

Let's have a closer look at these strategies. Being creative is often encouraged for anyone who struggles with mental health because it gives us a way of expressing ourselves that doesn't involve talking. It helps us to understand our own feelings or experiences once they are out of our minds. Your painting might look like a blob of colours on a canvas to others but to you it will tell part of your story. Check-in with yourself and see how you feel after you painted, drew or wrote about your illness. Do you feel better? Do your feelings make a bit more sense now? Or are you just exhausted and you are glad it is over?

Either of these scenarios is completely fine. Remember that the most important thing is that you TRIED to help yourself feel better. It's not a competition that requires specific results, and it's not about creating a masterpiece. When we live with mental health challenges, we often go through a lot of trial and error to find what works best. Some activities and strategies work really well for some but not for everyone. This can sound frustrating and it is at times. Remember - you are doing this for yourself. You deserve to find the right strategies and have every right to take your time to find what works best for you. We live in a rushed world and it always seems like we need top-notch results within minutes. There seems to be no room left to be 'wrong' or to reevaluate what we tried. When it comes to mental health – screw that. Big time.

Looking after our mental health can be time-consuming, and at times we don't see real results until days, weeks or maybe even years after something we have tried. It's hard to predict outcomes when we are constantly changing, our lives and circumstances change, and that makes outcomes variable. That is perfectly okay.

First and foremost, do yourself a favour and stop thinking you must achieve huge progress every day. Stop telling yourself that you *must* feel better today because you felt terrible for the last week. Instead, set yourself an achievable pace. This is your way of nurturing kindness towards yourself! We are so used to thinking that change should and will always be fast and easy. So, when we do decide to be kinder to ourselves, we expect to feel better instantly. That is kind of true; making that decision to nurture yourself can lift some of that heavy feeling straight away, but that is only the beginning of the process. True and deep change takes time, and part of getting used to living, breathing and exercising 'kindness', is to realise and accept that we can only be successful by following our path at our own pace.

As you go along, you will find some steps have not worked - but that is okay. Nothing is ever wasted when we approach it with kindness. This simply means you tried a strategy and found it didn't work for you. Focus on the fact that you tried something, not that you didn't get the result you had hoped for. Acknowledge that you want to feel better and be proud that you started the process to find your thing! Who cares if you don't like painting or the poem you wrote is not what you thought it would be? That is not important! Even if it seems like you failed, you haven't. Trying a strategy, even if it wasn't overly helpful, still helped you take another step towards recovery.

Let me also take a moment to discuss the following two strategies in depth – going outside and exercise.

This is certainly advice that many healthcare professionals would offer to you. I am listing it here because as annoying as it might be, these two really work and here's why. Being outside gives us the chance to ground ourselves. Grounding is a very powerful strategy to become calm and re-connect with our bodies and emotions when we're feeling anxious and depressed. Grounding requires us to pay attention to our senses. That is why walking outside in a forest, for example, will calm us down because our senses are gently stimulated which causes for our heartrate to become more regular, breathing becomes easier and 'happy' hormones are being released, causing for stress hormones to drop. That is why we DO feel better after spending time in the sun. I am not suggesting sunbaking at the beach until we get skin cancer. It is far healthier to go for a walk for 30 minutes and enjoy the sun that way. And that totally counts as exercise! Physical activity is one of the biggest challenges when we are depressed. We feel sluggish, run-down, drained and deprived of energy. To get out of bed, get dressed AND leave the house is a big ask, no doubt about it.

Start with small steps and build up from there. If you have a yard, take a few steps around it or walk to your letterbox and back. If you have a balcony, spend a few minutes outside on that. This might seem like nothing, but it is something and definitely a great start. It gets you used to being outside without having to talk to anyone. You can build up from these small actions and eventually, you will have your 30 minutes a day in the bag!

Being outside and in the sun is not always easy, especially in winter. That can be a real downer because depression tends to get worse in winter. Less sun can lead to fewer happy feelings. Walking in the rain under a grey sky can be very depressing; remember though, you are not expected to stay out there all day. Getting outside for just ten minutes on those days is plenty. It's also fine to just stay indoors sometimes; we are not Olympic athletes who must adhere to a vigorous exercise routine.

When it comes to mental health, we need to be guided by our feelings. If there are days where you feel like staying home and reading a good book or watching Netflix, that is fine. It is all about balance. The reason why health professionals mention exercise and being outside is simple – never going outside is detrimental to our mental health. Don't we know that already, though? Thanks, Captain Obvious! For those living with mental health challenges, our own four walls are often our one true safe space where we can just be. At the same time, the walls can close in on us at times and increase our loneliness and isolation. There is always a fine line, and it pays off to remind yourself of that from time to time.

Our environment plays a huge role in our mental wellbeing, and part of that is the weather. That is a simple fact. If you find it hard to get motivated to be outside in the colder months or just in general, then acknowledge that. It is what it is.

Always keep the following tips in mind:

DON'T

- Beat yourself up over it
- Feel like you failed
- Worry about the time spent inside

DO

- Remember today is a new day
- Remind yourself you are trying your best every day
- Be proud for trying again today
- Take it slowly
- Set yourself a little goal for the day – 10 minutes outside
- Focus on the present moment – yesterday doesn't matter

I know it can be hard to see a new day as a blessing when we are stuck in a rut, and the world is bleak. It is a challenge, but it is one you can master. All you have to do is – *start*.

Anxiety

> "Trust yourself. You've survived a lot, and you'll survive whatever is coming."
> Robert Tew

Anxiety – often mentioned, rarely understood properly. It has almost become a fashionable thing to have, which is insulting beyond words to those that struggle with it on a daily basis. Anxiety is not nice – it sucks.

You may have noticed I have given anxiety and depression separate chapters in this book. They often get mentioned in the same breath, and I can understand where that comes from. Anxiety and depression are similar – but they are not the same! Someone can suffer from depression but not from anxiety and vice versa. Some people get the double whammy and live with both.

It can be hard to get a diagnosis of anxiety, and it is often difficult for people to truly understand what suffering from it really means. Anxiety often gets confused as stress, and this is understandable to a point. Stress manifests in similar physical sensations to anxiety – heart racing, getting sweaty, feeling lightheaded and the overall feeling of being unwell and not quite right. In both cases, the body tries to tell us that something is going on, and it is not good; it wants us to rectify the situation.

The major difference is that stress is generally caused by external factors such as work, relationship matters or family emergencies. Anxiety is an internal response and causes the body to go into flight or fight mode which elevates our senses. We then either find a way to sort the situation out or we run away from it. That can be highly stressful, but it is not stress. We are dominated by feelings of fear, dread and apprehension. This is another difference between stress and anxiety. When we are stressed, we feel a wide range of emotions. We feel sad, angry, upset and/or worried. These emotions are not part of anxiety. Of course, we can feel worried, sad and upset as well, but that is BECAUSE we have anxiety; it is not caused by the anxiety itself. A small but important difference.

To better understand anxiety, it is worth learning what is going on in your body, most importantly in your brain when you experience it. You will know the tense sensation in your stomach, the heightened sense of awareness you have about anything going around you and that slight but growing fear or sense of dread. On a neurological level, there is even more going on. The brain is in full swing, and several parts of it are hard at work when you are experiencing anxiety, with the amygdala being in charge. It triggers the body to be flooded with hormones that boost perception, reflexes and speed in dangerous situations.

On a physical level, you might experience sweaty hands, dizziness, tension across your neck and shoulders, nausea, shallow breathing, numbness, tightness in the chest and/or your heart racing. This can be scary and discomforting because there is so much going on. Eventually, the initial fight or flight response eases and gets weaker. The brain realizes that there is no threat and it calls off the action. Things can return to normal, and you will know the anxiety attack (or the threat in your mind's idea of events) is over. We all can experience these kinds of events when we are in real danger and need to make a decision on what to do.

The above describes a one-time event. Anxiety or generalized anxiety disorder (GAD) doesn't stop at just one attack. It becomes a constant companion in people's lives. They tend to feel worried or anxious most of (or all) the time. They have triggers that can set off an attack, and these can happen several times a day, week or month. It is no longer a rare, one-time event. Anxiety can become somewhat predictable if sufferers are in tune with their triggers and know how to manage them. That is why anxiety is such a massive bitch, though. It often remains unpredictable and can fire up even if we think we have all of our triggers sorted. Our bodies are 'used' to being in a state of high alert, and sometimes it doesn't take much for the scales to tip and anxiety to swoop in and take over. A body that is used to anxiety becomes harder to regulate and keep calm.

That's the bad news, the good news is that it can be changed. Your mind and body can be trained to react differently, no matter your age. That is where your power lies. You CAN change how you respond to anxiety, and these responses can be updated, fine-tuned or discarded as you go along your journey. If anxiety can adapt to new life circumstances, then so can your brain. Anxiety is a very personal matter that presents itself uniquely to you. This means YOU will have to take notice of changes and triggers to decode your anxiety. This will help you discover the best management strategies for yourself. The key is to allow yourself to be kind. Let go of any notions that you must feel better immediately. You will feel better! It will be a gentler and more sustainable approach if you are doing so with kindness as your first choice. If we want to deal with our struggles effectively, we need less harsh self-judgment. We need to find a kinder way of looking at ourselves and the situations we find ourselves in.

Before we dive into some of the strategies you can use, I want to remind you that it is not helpful or healthy to compare your anxiety to others. Do not compare your level of anxiety to someone else's or think you should feel better because you only have 'some anxiety'. Thinking like that just blocks your road to recovery. This is not about other people; it is about YOU! All pain and struggle matter and that includes your anxiety and the unique way it presents itself. Remember this when you hit a roadblock or if someone tells you they found the 'best' way to deal with their anxiety. It is awesome if someone is successful with their chosen strategy - but let's not focus on what others do. You have your own path ahead of you and deserve to walk it at your own pace and rhythm.

This brings us to the dos and don'ts for anxiety. Again, feel free to add your own.

DON'T:

- Feel ashamed
- Let negative self-talk become your strongest voice
- Beat yourself up
- Do what others want you to do

DO:

- Focus on yourself
- Take your time
- Sort yourself out first
- Make your mental health a priority

Below are a few strategies that have proven helpful for people living with anxiety.

- Breathing exercises
- Practice mindfulness
- Remove yourself from the situation
- Talk to someone who understands
- Take prescribed medication
- Yoga
- Ground yourself in nature
- Exercise
- Spend time with animals and/or kids
- Essential oils
- Progressive muscle relaxation – tending and relaxing each muscle group of the body
- Cuddles
- Reading
- Colouring in
- Meditation
- Talk yourself through it using positive language
- Say irrational thoughts out loud
- Say No
- Remember that progress isn't straightforward

This list is not complete. Many things will work for different people. It is important to remember; routine is often the key to keeping anxiety at bay. This can mean that you have daily activities that help take your mind off things and unwind from the day, such as reading or colouring in. When you find something that works well for you, it is worthwhile making it into a habit.

Routine gives us predictability – something that in itself is highly effective to combat something as unpredictable as anxiety. It gives us peace of mind and comfort. So, don't feel bad if you stick to a routine that helps you. Don't apologise for it and don't cancel it simply because someone wants you to go out for dinner instead. You can tweak a routine of course but don't change a winning strategy for outside influences.

Let's also look at something that many people tend to overlook – human touch. Anxiety may prevent some of us being amongst big groups of people, but that doesn't mean we should deprive ourselves of human connection. Physical touch can be very calming, reassuring and comforting. When it comes from the right person, human touch is kindness in its purest form. It allows us to be vulnerable in a safe place, and to be loved for who we are right at that moment. Deep, meaningful human connection is what kindness thrives on and allows it to grow roots in our hearts and souls. Make sure to get a cuddle from someone you trust so the physical connection will actually help you and not agitate further.

For some people, touch or physical closeness can just be too much, even more so when they are experiencing an anxiety attack. That does not mean you don't appreciate their effort, but it is not helpful if it agitates you further. The best time to talk to loved ones about how they can help effectively is when you feel calm. Perhaps you can come up with a signal to communicate with one another for when you are having an anxiety attack? It may be hard for you to get words out, but if you lift one particular finger, your loved one will know that you need a bit of space. Lift two fingers to indicate that you feel a little better and are ready for them to be close to you. Of course, these are just suggestions. I encourage you to have this conversation with your partner and/or other loved ones; and work together to come up with your own signals.

The techniques mentioned here have one thing in common – they are designed to encourage you to focus on something else, hence reducing the anxiety. This is often the winning ticket. Most of these techniques also need very little or no equipment, which is even better!

It is important to point out how damaging negative or irrational thoughts are. On the other side, using positive language can help you to talk yourself through an anxiety attack. We can NOT underestimate the power of words, either in our thoughts or spoken out loud. Depending on the type of words you use, they can enhance an attack or help to end it. If you feel an attack coming on and don't think you can use positive language throughout, don't worry. There is an effective technique that demands less focus on the language you use and it's part of the Grounding strategy using our senses once more.

Look around the room or space you are in. Name five green things you can see. The colour here is interchangeable and only serves as an example. Make sure to say, 'I see one green cup, one green flower, one green tablecloth' and so on. Next, look around and find shapes. Is there a square table, a rectangular window or a round table? Examine the room and say out loud once more what you are seeing. You can also look for contrasts in the room (bright/dark or clean/dirty, just as examples) and name them. Ideally, you can name these things out loud. Of course, in a room full of people, you might not want to draw attention to yourself by naming objects and shapes out loud. You can also do it quietly in your head.

The main trick behind this technique is that you are firing up different parts of your brain to complete this task. These areas would not be activated during an anxiety attack. This is because other parts of your brain are busy taking centre stage. Our mind can be manipulated though, and if you 'force' the attention to be elsewhere, the brain starts to redirect attention to areas of the brain that are not in charge of strong emotions, fight or flight scenarios or flooding your body with different hormones. Your brain might not be excited about this technique when you first start using it. We are creatures of habit after all so it might take a few attempts for this to work for you. It may seem daunting but look at it this way - with every attempt, you are getting better at managing your anxiety and getting to know yourself better! No attempt at this is ever wasted or pointless; remember, it takes time to develop a new habit. Most importantly, you are helping yourself and taking small steps towards feeling better.

There is another important thing to address when trying to fight off an anxiety attack. Quite often, we focus on breathing and trying to slow down our breath to calm down. This is often highly effective, and such a great tool to use! In some cases, breathing exercises don't bring the result we are hoping for. For people who have suffered trauma that includes physical assault and/or injuries, focusing on breathing can be a trigger, not a solution. In some cases, trauma memories can be carried in the face, neck or chest – parts of the body where the breath flows through when we practice breathing exercises. If that is you, that is absolutely fine. There are other ways you can ground yourself and focus on your awareness away from your anxiety.

Activating other senses such as smell, or hearing might offer the ideal solution to help manage your anxiety. Smells have been proven to affect our emotions, both positively and negatively. It is important to note that certain smells can trigger trauma survivors and induce an anxiety attack. At the same time, smells can be calming, such as the smell of rain or trees. If you find that certain smells help to calm you down, definitely try this method. If you can, spend time in the environment that produces this smell (such as a forest or the beach). If you can't get to one of those places, try recreating it at home in your safe space. When you work with essential oils, know that less is more; they are very potent and can become overpowering. Don't go overboard with them, but definitely use them if you find a certain smell has a calming effect on you.

Although we live in a very visual world, our sense of hearing can also be used to help manage anxiety. Repetitive sounds often work well - such as waves, the sound of a fan in your room or listening to a simple drum beat. Music can do the trick too, as long as you play calm and gentle tunes - this is not the time for loud music. As we listen to calming sounds, our breathing will slow down, but we are not necessarily aware of it.

All of the suggested techniques offer ways to activate parts of the brain that are in shut down mode as anxiety takes over. To find what works for you, allow yourself to explore what the different senses mean to you. Don't judge yourself if you struggle with using smell or sounds to calm yourself. Look at it with kindness – if it won't work for you, that is fine. It is what it is. Let yourself be guided by kindness and not harsh judgment. Kindness will show you the way to the strategy that works best for you.

Self-doubt

> "Your self-doubt does not define who you are or what you are capable of"
> Unknown

Self-doubt feels a bit like a Pandora's box. We are often reluctant to examine and address it because we fear that everything will unravel once it comes to the surface. Self-doubt is tricky like that. It can sneak up on us quickly and then take over completely. The good news is – you can stop that from happening. It will take some time and constant work before self-doubt is where it belongs – far away from your thought processes and wellbeing.

In this chapter, I want to give you some tips on how to address self-doubt quickly. In particular, what you can do when you are about to do something important, like a job interview perhaps or a presentation at uni. Many people tend to think self-doubt is very complex and will take ages to overcome. Some are even convinced it will never go away. These are valid thoughts.

Self-doubt is the crown jewel in the crown of our social conditioning. It has been used heavily, often in correlation with shame, to make us believe that we are no good, that we can't do anything right and that we are such failures in life. It is a powerful tool that has helped many generations to keep us at bay and subdued and to never ask for too much. So, in that regard, yes, it will take a long time to overcome (anyone in the mood for bringing down the patriarchy?)

Despite the hurdles in front of us, we can tackle self-doubt in our daily lives. It doesn't have to be complicated; it starts with one simple but important step – yep, you guessed it. It's kindness. Self-doubt is a very powerful enemy and is often very successful in drowning out kindness. Together with shame, it's the main culprit that stops us changing course and allowing kindness into our self-care regime. Self-doubt causes the voice in your head to say 'Just look at you with all these flaws; you are not worthy of receiving kindness, even from yourself. You don't even know how!'

Self-doubt can deliver several knockout blows within seconds; it is a very cocky and arrogant opponent. It is used to following the same path, and that makes it vulnerable. Self-doubt has little room to manipulate us when we start to change the narrative about ourselves. As you build up your tolerance and openness to kindness, self-doubt weakens with every attempt you take to be kinder to yourself.

Self-doubt, much like shame, is based on habit. Admittedly, it is a powerful habit because lots of us have grown up not feeling good enough and worthy. But kindness is patient. It is ready to be built up whenever you are ready. It doesn't matter if you are 5 years old or 35 or 55. It is there to help you and take over for the better once you choose to change paths. Let's give it a go and kick self-doubt to where it belongs – the curb.

Below are a few strategies to use and I recommend using them daily; even on a good day. As we learned in the chapter about anxiety, it pays to make a habit out of a successful routine or ritual. It never hurts to look at yourself in the mirror when washing your hands. Use this time to talk to yourself quietly – or out loud if you prefer; whatever works for you! So here we go:

- Talk yourself up making sure to use positive words only

Tell yourself you *can* do this instead of thinking you can't. Remind yourself that you rock and are amazing; that you prepared well for this presentation - or that you have all of the skills and assets required to a potential new job! Be nice to yourself.

- Breathe

Breathe deeply and slowly. Focus on your breath, then inhale and exhale. Repeat this a few times and close your eyes if you can. When you pay attention to your breath, you not only shut out the world around you and its distractions, but you also keep the negative self-talk at bay. If concentrating on your breathing isn't working for you, switch to your other senses such as smell or vision. Taking the time to inhale a lovely scent can give you something different to focus on - essential oils, a fragrant candle or even flowers from your garden. You can also try looking for some small and unexpected beauty, either somewhere inside your home, or by going for a walk.

- Take your time

Keeping your anxiety on a short leash will help to reduce or even stop the self-doubt. Those two often work closely together, which really sucks. Don't despair, they are also known to vanish together when you tell them to bugger off. The kindest thing you can do for yourself is to take your time. Don't rush through your presentation, try to slow yourself down before you answer a question in a job interview. When we rush, our speech can become unclear; our breathing can become shallow, and our heart rate goes up. Before you know it, self-doubt has settled back into your mind. Take your time; you have every right to.

These techniques are great to fall back on. For long-term success to abolish self-doubt, it pays to put strategies in place long before the pressure is on.

When we first start to tackle self-doubt, it requires work. This can be daunting, and that is okay! The trick is to know self-doubt's weakness – habit.

Self-doubt is a lazy bitch in many ways. It has its own routines and sticks to them stubbornly. It makes a habit of rearing its head at certain times, and its favourite will be the worst possible time for you. Unlike anxiety, it is predictable, and you can see it coming. Think of a situation that triggers your self-doubt. Perhaps it pops up when you're asked to do something you have never done before. Does it appear when you have to do something you haven't done in a while? Your first reaction might be 'I can't do that. I don't know/can't remember how to. I will fail.' These are courtesy of your self-doubt.

The good thing is though that self-doubt only puts up as much resistance as you allow it to. The trick is to shut it down before it gets a chance to do its routine. This is where the 'work' comes in. To kick self-doubt to the curb, work on it as often as you can, including on your good days. It's best to set up a daily routine full of positivity that works for you.

There are a few suggested dos and don'ts on the following pages. You will find blank space at the end of each so you can add to them if you want to.

DO:

- Set a positive intention for the day when you wake up (Today will be a good day, today will rock!)
- Remind yourself of your intention throughout the day
- Write positive reminders on little notes and leave them at your desk or similar place at work, home, etc.
- Have a positive picture or quote as your screensaver for your phone or computer
- Finish the day grateful – think about five things you were grateful for that day
- Be proud of what you achieved on the day

DON'T:

- Be hard on yourself if self-doubt creeps up on you
- Think the day is ruined entirely if you encounter self-doubt
- Stop what you are doing – keep going!
- Dwell on a potential step backwards – it's a setback, not the end of it all

Most importantly, you will have good days where you are on top of your self-doubt. On other days, it will be harder to keep the lid on the cranky little beast. That's okay - nobody is perfect. This is not about being perfect; it is about reclaiming your space and defining which thoughts can reside in your head and getting rid of those that are not welcome. It will get easier with time and practice (The 'work,' I mentioned earlier.). Self-doubt will become smaller and more insignificant. As mentioned previously, kindness is patient and non-judgmental. It doesn't matter if we have bad days. Kindness is ready to start fresh the next day. Remember, if you have had a bad day or a day you consider unsuccessful, it is just a day. You can start again tomorrow and allow kindness back into the driver's seat.

It's all about trying! The one big thing on your side is that every day provides the opportunity to start again. If yesterday was crappy, that doesn't matter today; it's a new day with brand new possibilities. Keep on trying!

Before we wrap up this chapter, we must have a chat about positive self-talk. It is crucial for a successful fight against self-doubt and to nurture and grow meaningful kindness. It is almost the very essence of it. It is also not very well known how powerful it is. It almost gets repetitive, but our social conditioning doesn't allow us to be kind to ourselves. We are trained to be so hard on ourselves all the time. It almost seems as though womanhood equals eternal suffering for being not good enough.

Although nobody says it out loud, and it is certainly not a law - it is universally known that women have doubts about their abilities and talents. So, when we are suddenly encouraged to talk about ourselves positively, it comes as a huge shock! We can't do that! We readily give compliments to our partners, children and friends on their achievements and unique talents but refer to ourselves as disgusting, a failure, unworthy, ugly and much more. We are not thin enough, not tall enough, not blond enough, and not pretty enough. It is fucked up!

Positive self-talk is so important! Do you use positive words when you talk to friends or family members? You also need to use them when talking about, or to yourself. Tell yourself you are fucking awesome and perfect; acknowledge to yourself when you put a lot of hard work into something - you deserve some fucking praise! Do this daily, all day every day! If you notice negative thoughts creeping in, stop yourself and change it up. We must, must, must change our own narratives. Start off small to get used to the change and build up your skill. It is an entirely new skill for most of us. We are such pros at being harsh and unforgiving toward ourselves, so being nice and kind instead will feel weird at first.

Below are the first few actions to do every day. You can add your own if you wish.

- Compliment yourself once a day
- Put a summary for your daily achievements together
- Take time to pat yourself on the back
- Allow yourself to feel awesome
- Decide to know that you are enough – right here, right now
- Remind yourself that you are perfect the way you are

- Don't compromise when it really doesn't suit you
- Let your fucking light shine

Self-care

Given this whole book is about caring for ourselves first with kindness, you might wonder why there is a chapter here dedicated to self-care? Firstly, it is because self-care is so important to help change the world that it deserves all of our attention. Secondly, self-care has finally started to become popular, and rightly so. For us to be fully well, we need and deserve to incorporate self-care into our daily lives. There is one thing we must address though, and that is how self-care is often perceived!

Self-care is often portrayed as an indulgence, a one-off thing or something you only do occasionally. For some reason, people often believe we should not indulge in something good and healing every day. We get told in blog posts and articles that we deserve to go to the spa and treat ourselves! Unfortunately, it often adds that we should only do that every now and then. This makes it appear as though self-care is all well and good - as long as we restrain ourselves and don't go crazy with it.

Painting self-care in that light misses the point of it entirely; it is not indulgent, it is necessary! In fact, for self-care to be successful and effective, we need to plan for it and believe it is important for everyday life. We should consider self-care as a must-do for staying alive, like breathing, eating and resting. This will encourage us to make a lot more room for it. Self-care is the much mentioned 'me' time. Instead of doing it just every now and then, or when it fits in with other people's schedules, we must practise it every single day.

So, how do we do practice self-care that goes beyond the glossy idea of spa days, getting a haircut and having a nice dinner alone? Don't get me wrong, these things can and should be part of self-care, but lasting self-care needs to go deeper than that. It starts with a change in our mindset. That change also needs to go beyond thinking you deserve self-care and that self-care is not selfish. These statements are absolutely true! It is also true that we can't pour from an empty cup. This is important to remember, especially people who often tend to keep on giving without expecting anything in return because they are very nurturing by nature. Don't get me wrong, nurturing is important! Without nurturing and loving care and protection, we all would have ended up like coldhearted arseholes. So, let's never down talk nurturing – it is a GOOD thing!

Unfortunately, many people take advantage of those who are nurturers. They are givers by nature, and selfish people often take this as an invitation to have nurturers do their bidding. You might have guessed it – people with a nurturing nature often suffer from depression and/or anxiety. It's the price they pay for being there for others who don't always deserve it. That is exactly why we must change our mindset about self-care. It shouldn't be considered as an occasional indulgent thing to do. It is time we saw it as a necessary process, one that we can draw from whenever we need extra strength and resources.

Deeply beneficial self-care is not always easy, but it is extremely worthwhile. When you find yourself feeling run down, and struggling to get through the day, it is time for more than minimal self-care. This is when you need more in-depth self-care. That, in short, is therapy. To make sure we keep our cup full, we need to know ourselves inside out. We need to set boundaries; nurturers often don't as it simply doesn't occur to them. How can they spend time on themselves when there is so much need for help in the world? That might be a noble thought, but it is quite destructive - you can't pour from an empty cup. It is impossible to continue caring for others if you don't take care of yourself.

Looking at ourselves is not always easy. It might bring up ugly memories and things that were hard to cope with. It is important to fight through that. You deserve to feel better; you deserve to keep nurturing and caring for yourself. It needs to be in a way that does not harm you. That is where therapy comes in. It doesn't necessarily mean that you will attend therapy for years; not at all. This is about getting to know yourself on a deeper level, deciding where your boundaries are, and then looking at how you can help others. AFTER you have helped yourself.

Self-care is important for everyone; those who struggle with depression and/or anxiety need it, even more, to help them to keep going. Those who suffer from self-doubt need it to keep that nasty bugger in check. We all need to care for ourselves - simply because we deserve it. We deserve to be content; we deserve to take time out – from worrying, struggling, fighting and surviving.

Let's just cut the bullshit and put yourself first for once – in a meaningful way.

Self-care is about recharging and doing something that is good for us but does not hurt others. We are taking CARE of ourselves; we are not being selfish. That is important to remember.

What should you do for effective self-care?

DO:

- Attend therapy
- Plan your self-care time ahead
- Stick to your plan

- Switch off (phone, laptop, etc., your mind)
- Do something that makes you feel good (here's the spa day, etc.)
- Change things up where you feel the need
- Check in with yourself to ensure you are doing something that is helping you
- Ignore those who think they know better

DON'T:

- Stop caring for yourself because you feel bad or pressured
- Listen to anyone who wants to take self-care time away from you
- Justify self-care to anyone
- Ever think you are not worthy of self-care

Now, you might wonder if therapy is the only option for successful self-care. Nope, it isn't - but it certainly doesn't hurt to try it. The benefits we get from it can make a huge difference to our wellbeing. Of course, there are other ways you can get to know yourself better besides therapy. You can gain a deeper understanding of your wants and needs, and how you can tend to them in a healing and meaningful manner. For self-care to be truly successful, we require a deep understanding of our personal needs and desires as well as where we don't fulfil them and why. This may seem a bit tedious to you, and that is okay - in a way it is. Self-care that is healing and lasting is a new discipline that we need to develop. Initially, it requires a strict approach as we learn to tune out distractions and negative thoughts. Although it might come across as tough love, it is not. It is a deep love for the self that we are uncovering, and I believe I am providing you with some powerful tools to do just that.

Always remember – investing time on healing yourself and self-care is NOT selfish. That fact will never change. As you dive deeper into self-care and commit to it at a whole new level, this is even more important to know and hold dear. The key to it is time and patience. Time, because it is not always easy to face up to the things we have been hiding from for so long, things we would often prefer to forget. It also takes time to believe that effective and deeply meaningful self-care comes from a place of worthiness and of knowing that we are enough.

This is where patience comes in. As women especially, we tend to brush these things away quickly because deep down, we feel unworthy of doing something life-changing for ourselves. We may have tried half-heartedly repeating, 'I am enough I am enough, I am enough, okay, done.' This could be because we are uneasy using positive self-talk. It also could be that we are not used to allowing ourselves to think about how worthy we are of putting our own wellbeing first. Only with practice and patience can we change things. It may feel weird at first because we are once again going against social conditioning.

Therefore, it is important to start with small steps and ease yourself into self-care that doesn't allow compromises. It will always be there and at the same time, you can still fulfil your nurturing duties. One does not have to negate the other! In the future, there can be no more or at least fewer occasions of missing out on things that are good for YOU in favour of someone else's needs.

What do these small steps look like?

- Set aside 5 minutes for yourself at the same time each day
- Start by consciously honouring these five minutes
- Be fully present in the moment during these 5 minutes
- Focus on your breathing
- Just be

Important points to make these five minutes successful:

- Don't think about things you should be doing
- Don't try and reorganize your to-do list
- Don't use the time to plan the rest of your day
- Don't look at your phone, tablet, laptop, etc.
- Don't have any loud and/or distracting noises around you

Five minutes might not seem like much for most, but for busy women, no minute can be left unused these days. We feel like we have to do everything, and somehow 24 hours in a day never seems to be enough.

Therefore, it is a HUGE deal to consciously make time for yourself for at least 5 minutes every single day at the same time!

The idea is to build from the five minutes and expand to a time frame that works best for you. It should really be 15 minutes minimum and needs to become your new normal - like eating and breathing. These 15 minutes, (or more) must be a time where you put yourself first. Unplug, take a breather, slow down and simply be you. Shut out the world and its noises and demands. Check-in with yourself and let your thoughts drift.

We have become so used to always functioning at our highest level to deliver what other people need. This often leads us to feel as though we just cannot have 15 minutes to ourselves. Even when we are exhausted after a long day at work, we stay up late to make sure everyone else's needs are met. We bake cookies for our children's school bake sale because we feel pressured into showing we can do everything with ease. We need to fight back on these expectations and pressures by claiming our time and self-worth back. Hell yes, school bake sales are important!

So are your kid's soccer games, hubby's office party and your policy meeting at work. I am not suggesting they should be pushed aside and forgotten. It is very important to change our thought process so that we remember it is okay to give priority to our own needs sometimes. There is nothing wrong with allowing ourselves time to recharge or giving some focus to our own desires. This is what deeply meaningful self-care targets. It is time for us to start our own personal revolution by taking 15 minutes for ourselves each day. We need to do this without excuses, compromise or the need for approval for others.

As you make daily self-care a new routine and then habit, there is room for you to create the time slot the way you want it to be. That can include meditating, yoga, going for a walk or spending time in a beloved bookshop. Or it can just be sitting somewhere comfortable to zone out and slow down. You can change it up each day if that works better, of course! The most important thing is to take time every day unapologetically for yourself. Of course, long days at the spa, a weekend or night away and any 'longer' activities still count as self-care and should be practiced as well. The daily self-care doesn't take away from that. It sets the foundation for it.

Receiving help

For people who thrive on helping others and are new to applying the same kind of attention to themselves, the following problem will sound familiar. We are shit at asking for help! And we are even worse at receiving help! It seems as if that is just not part of our DNA. WE are the ones that help others. WE are the ones who give, but we refuse to be on the other end of that equation. This is something that absolutely must change. Part one of being able to look after ourselves is what we have discussed throughout this book – putting ourselves first and practising kindness towards ourselves first and foremost.

Part two of self-care and self-love, the kind that lasts and uplifts and nourishes your mental health, is to receive help. It might sound stupid, but it really isn't that easy. There is a fine art to just saying 'Thank you' and gratefully receiving what has been offered. Instead, we say 'Thank you, but you really shouldn't have.' or 'Thank you, but I really don't deserve this.' We often blush, feel uncomfortable and just want all the attention gone.

My dear, this is so sweet and says so much about you. You are just too good for this world at times, aren't you? We need to preserve that quality of yours, and one way to do exactly that is for you to start receiving help. How does that look like in reality? It can be a small thing, such as letting someone unpack groceries for you. When someone offers to let you go before them in the queue at the supermarket, go ahead and go first; or you can let a friend buy you a cup of coffee. These are actually great opportunities to practice how to receive by saying 'Thank you' or 'That's very kind of you'. It's time to drop the I don't deserve this. You do!

Receiving help goes hand in hand with asking for help. That is a challenge for many of us. You might feel bad when asking for help or believe you should really be able to do it yourself. You don't need help because you are a one-woman super show, and no one can help you satisfactorily anyway. I get it – it IS hard to receive help and even harder to ask for it.

Here is some good news for you though, you don't have to ask for help all the time. It is not about the quantity of help, but the quality. If you ask for help just once a year and it helps you immensely, that is perfect. If you end up receiving help every month, that is wonderful. This is all about what works for YOU. You not only deserve to make your mental wellbeing a priority, but also to communicate your needs and then to receive the help to have them met. We are the eternal multi-taskers and don't expect any praise for it. That is why we are the ones who hold the family together, and everyone depends on it. Being the centre of the family universe is a great position to be in. This is not about changing that, quite the opposite. It is about strengthening that position, so it remains sustainable, and you can keep being the superwoman that you truly are.

So, let's look at how we can start implementing this change and incorporate receiving help into your life.

The first thing to remember is that YOU are in control. YOU decide what kind of help you will accept. The challenge is for you to be open to receiving help without giving up control over what is important to you. What we need to do is break down the resistance within you that keeps you from taking care of yourself fully, and to encourage you to accept help every now and then. You need to learn to do this without feeling guilty.

Quite often, we feel weak when we realise we need help. It is such a common thought in society at large – men don't ask for help or cry because they believe it will make them look weak. Women have been taught that they don't have the right to ask for help. If we do, we feel as though we must apologise for failing to meet expectations. So, we don't make it easy for anyone to ask for help, and we have never encouraged people to feel good about receiving it. So, it is no surprise that we feel a lot of resistance to receiving help. And because we are always so focused on helping others, we might not even be aware that our mental health is suffering. This is because we ignore our need for help.

So how do we change it? By taking small steps. Ask for help with something simple first. Maybe there is a cake stall at school, and you are expected to contribute something. Is there someone who could help you with that; do you have a friend that really enjoys baking and would be happy to whip something up? This example might sound silly, but it is a simple way to reach out and ask for help. The thing is, you are still on safe ground – you are still in control. You are merely outsourcing something small while the big picture is still looking good. We can also start building from a small request like this, and it can take you in any direction you want. You might end up with a regular cleaner for your household. Perhaps you will discover that going to see a therapist once a fortnight is an excellent way to debrief and let go. If we don't receive 'small' help and get comfortable with it, 'big' help will be impossible to accept.

We also need to redefine what help really means to us. We have been led to believe that needing help means we failed at something, right? Nope, that is wrong! It simply means that we need help. For some reason, we seem to add judgment to it. Needing help is needing help, period. You deserve it and have every right to receive it. Start believing that needing help is something you are worthy of. You deserve to breathe a bit easier; you have every right to have energy left to look after your mental health. You deserve to be able to be the best YOU that you can be. The ways and means you are doing it are yours to choose.

Start immediately and try to receive today; just something small. Then build up from there. Receiving help can be incredibly empowering. It sets free new energy, new ideas and new paths. You deserve to keep evolving and growing. Putting yourself first by receiving help is not selfish – it is much needed. It will make you an even better person with an even bigger heart and kinder attitude. Start today and see where it will take you! I can't wait for you to explore new things because you changed something small but significant – simply by realizing that you deserve to receive help.

Epilogue

After everything is said and done

This is it! We have come to the end of our journey on how to apply kindness to yourself. I hope you feel empowered and inspired. Kindness is often so simple yet so powerful. Of course, kindness is not a new concept. Many wise men and women have talked about it for centuries. Many religions have it in their 'rulebooks' on how to live a good life. I am grateful for that, but I know we can take it further.

Kindness is unlimited. We can and must show it to everyone, regardless of their gender, race, identity, religious belief or background. Our minds often make life unnecessarily complicated and hard. Kindness comes from the heart and can be spontaneous, crazy and beautiful. We need and deserve kindness in our daily life, so we are ready to go out there to change this hurting world for the better.

This doesn't mean our time is wasted if we don't achieve something grand every day. When we're guided by kindness, we feel at peace and more at ease. Just by being ourselves, we can make someone's day better. That's what it's all about. If someone goes home happier because they interacted with a kind person, or somebody received a random act of kindness, then we succeeded.

Growing and nurturing is not about reinventing the wheel. It is about stopping the wheel that has spun out of control; it is energized by hatred, greed and ignorance. We can and must fight that every day with kindness.

So, here's to you and your kindness. I know you will grow it, nurture it and own the shit out of it. Here's to a better and kinder world, and to achieving it one kind word, one kind action, and one kind thought at a time.

Glossary

Techniques explained further

Throughout this book, I have mentioned techniques that are suitable for different situations and mental health challenges. I wanted to elaborate a bit further on them for people who might be new to them or have heard of them but are not sure what they actually mean. Words like 'meditation' and 'mindfulness' are thrown around easily these days, although not everyone knows what they mean.

Meditation

Meditation is not so much what we DO but rather what we ARE. It is a state we want to reach through practice. In that state, we are not enslaved by our thoughts and the often-negative emotions that come with it. Thoughts such as: 'I am not good enough', 'I have to do this or that or, I am such a failure'. This list could go on forever. Such thoughts are very stress-inducing; they make us feel inadequate and insecure. They can trigger our anxiety, self-doubt and/or depression. Meditation stops those thoughts and behaviours and hence reduces stress levels. The culprit of this stress-inducing behavior is the mind. We become what we think. If we think about negative things or emotions, we attract negative things and emotions into our lives. Meditation is a great way to stop that and allows us to put our minds into its place. Don't get me wrong; the mind is a powerful tool – as long as it is used correctly.

Meditation can be an effective form of stress reduction and has the potential to improve quality of life and decrease health care costs. Meditation involves achieving a state of 'thoughtless awareness' in which the excessive stress producing activity of the mind is neutralized without reducing alertness and effectiveness.

Many people think of mediation as a moment where they sit quietly and ponder their thoughts. Meditation is not about thoughts and examining them. Mediation is a state of awareness without thoughts.

We don't meditate to mull over an issue we have or to gain thoughtful insights into the world's problems. Thoughts are not important when meditating, in fact, they are distracting. Of course, the mind will not just switch off when it is asked to - it likes to be active. This is where a meditation class or step by step program comes in highly useful. It takes time and patience to get into the swing of things, but once you are, you will get the full benefits of mediation.

There are plenty of great resources online to get you started, and many of them are free. It pays to do some research to find the right fit for you. Start with something simple and see where it takes you.

Mindfulness

Mindfulness is another popular term that is often used, but not always understood. Just like meditation, mindfulness is a great tool for anyone who wants to catch a break from a mind going wild. Mindfulness is similar to meditation, which is why they are often mentioned in the same breath. While meditation aims to reach a state of thoughtless awareness, mindfulness is about being fully present 'in' the moment. When we are practising mindfulness, we are aware of where we are and what we are doing. We do so without being overwhelmed by what is going on around us. That is the reason mindfulness is suggested so often; it allows us to calm down so we can continue what we are doing with less or no anxiety.

There are many ways to practice mindfulness. It can be as simple as taking a breath and remembering your many strengths; hence pushing negative thoughts and overwhelming emotions away. It can be practised in a class or at home, preferably daily at a set time. The trick is to find something that works for you. Just like meditation, there are many free resources available online.

Social conditioning

Social conditioning is the process of training individuals in society to have certain beliefs; behaviours, desires and emotional reactions. These are approved by society in general, or by certain groups within it. We experience social conditioning from the moment we are born, and it continues throughout childhood and our teenage years. Social conditioning also occurs as adults as we enter different stages of life. We get conditioned by our parents, teachers, peers, people living in our community, the media, religious institutions and through information read in books, online, etc.

Now, social conditioning is not bad per se as it can help us make sense of the world. It becomes questionable when it impacts negatively on people and how they live their lives. All too often, it forces us into a certain behaviour because it appears as though only specific behaviour is acceptable. Another danger of social conditioning is that it works best when it is continually repeated, and then gets rewarded. A classic example is how girls are given positive attention IF they behave exactly how an adult wants them to. Therefore, they learn they can only get attention by doing what others expect them to, and not what they want to do. With that comes the understanding that as women, we must be submissive and put ourselves last. This obviously interferes with giving the appropriate time to good and meaningful self-care let alone nurturing kindness.

Some other harmful forms of social conditioning are that mental illness is something to be ashamed of, being encouraged not to talk about anything relating to death or that boys should not cry. This list could go on for days, but I think these give you the general idea of what I'm talking about.

About the Author

Karin Holmes is an author and counsellor, specialising in grief counselling and mental health support. She is passionate about helping people heal in a deep, meaningful and kind way. Hence this book! Karin lives in Canberra, Australia, with her two children.

www.karinholmes.com

www.ingramcontent.com/pod-product-compliance
Lightning Source LLC
Chambersburg PA
CBHW050317010526
44107CB00055B/2279